Grade 3

The Syllabus of Examination requirements, especially those sight-reading. Attention should Notices on the front inside c of changes.

The syllabus is obtainable from music dealers or from The Associated Board of the Royal Schools of Music, 14 Bedford Square, London WC1B 3JG (please send a stamped addressed C5 envelope).

In overseas centres, information may be obtained from the Local Representative or Resident Secretary.

Requirements

SCALES, ARPEGGIOS AND BROKEN CHORDS
(from memory)

Scales

(i) in similar motion, hands together one octave apart, and each hand separately, in the following keys: A, E, B, B♭, E♭ majors and B, G, C minors (melodic *or* harmonic minor at candidate's choice) (all two octaves)

(ii) in contrary motion, both hands beginning and ending on the key-note (unison), in the keys of A and E♭ majors (two octaves)

Chromatic Scales

each hand separately, beginning on A♭, B and C (two octaves)

Arpeggios

the common chords of A, E, B, B♭ and E♭ majors, and B, G and C minors, in root position only, each hand separately (two octaves)

Broken Chords

formed from the chords of G and F majors, and E and D minors, each hand separately, according to *either* of the patterns shown in the syllabus at candidate's choice

PLAYING AT SIGHT (see current syllabus)

AURAL TESTS (see current syllabus)

THREE PIECES

LIST A		page
1	**George Frideric Handel** (1685–1759) Gavotte in G, HWV 491	2
2	**František Xaver Dušek** (1731–1799) Andante grazioso: Sonata in F, second movement	3
3	**Carl Nielsen** (1865–1931) 'Marziale', No. 7 from *Piano Music for Young and Old*, Op. 53	4

LIST B		
1	**Georg Philipp Telemann** (1681–1767) Allegro in E minor	5
2	**Génari Karganov** (1858–1890) Little Waltz, Op. 25 No. 3	6
3	**Béla Bartók** (1881–1945) 'Lento', No. 11 from *For Children*, Vol. I	8

Candidates must prepare Nos. 1 & 2 from the *same* list, A *or* B, but may choose No. 3 from *either* list *or* one of the further alternatives listed below:

B. Godard See-Saw (Balancelle), Op. 149 Book 1 No. 4
Kabalevsky Clowns, Op. 39 No. 20
These are included in A Romantic Sketchbook for Piano, Book II, *published by the Associated Board*

Editor for the Associated Board: **Richard Jones**

© 1997 by The Associated Board of the Royal Schools of Music

No part of this publication may be copied or reproduced in any form or by any means without the prior permission of the publishers.

Music origination by Barnes Music Engraving Ltd.
Printed in Great Britain by Headley Brothers Ltd, The Invicta Press, Ashford, Kent and London.

Where appropriate, pieces have been checked with original source material and edited as necessary for instructional purposes. Fingering, phrasing, pedalling, metronome marks and the editorial realization of ornaments (where given) are for guidance but are not comprehensive or obligatory.

Gavotte in G

HWV 491

HANDEL

Source: London, British Library, R.M. 19.a.4. (c.1732).
Despite its title this piece is, in style, more like a bourrée than a gavotte. It is thought to date from around 1705 when Handel was a young man living and working in Hamburg. The slurs of bars 2 and 12–15 are present in the source; the remaining slurs and the dynamics and ornaments are editorial suggestions only. Unmarked crotchets may be lightly detached.

© 1997 by The Associated Board of the Royal Schools of Music
Selected from Handel, *Selected Keyboard Works*, Book I, edited by Richard Jones (Associated Board)

Andante grazioso
Second movement from Sonata in F

A:2

F. X. DUŠEK

František Xaver Dušek (1731–99) was an exact contemporary of Joseph Haydn and one of the most outstanding Bohemian composers of his day. In this slow movement the repeat of bars 1–8 has been notated in full.

© 1997 by The Associated Board of the Royal Schools of Music

Marziale

No. 7 from *Piano Music for Young and Old*, Op. 53

A:3

Edited by
Lionel Salter

NIELSEN

© Copyright 1930 by Skandinavisk og Borups Musikforlag
Reprinted by permission of Edition Wilhelm Hansen/Chester Music Ltd, for use only in connection with the examinations of the Royal Schools of Music. All enquiries for this piece apart from the examinations should be addressed to Chester Music Ltd, 8/9 Frith Street, London W1V 5TZ.

AB 2591

Allegro in E minor

TELEMANN

Source: *Fugues légères et petits jeux à clavessin seul* (Hamburg, *l'auteur*, 1738/9).
The Allegro is the finale of the fifth group of pieces. The repeat of bars 1–8, indicated by repeat marks in the source, is here notated in full. Unslurred quavers may be detached. Slurs and dynamics are editorial suggestions only.

© 1997 by The Associated Board of the Royal Schools of Music

B:2

Little Waltz
Op. 25 No. 3

KARGANOV

© 1983 by The Associated Board of the Royal Schools of Music
Reprinted from Karganov, *Album for the Young*, Op. 25 (Associated Board)

B:3

Lento

No. 11 from *For Children*, Vol. I

BARTÓK

Revised edition © Copyright 1946 by Boosey & Hawkes Inc., New York. Publishers for Germany, Austria, Hungary, Romania, the Czech Republic, Slovakia, Poland, Bulgaria, Albania, China and the former territories of Yugoslavia and the USSR: Editio Musica Budapest. For all other countries: Boosey & Hawkes Music Publishers Ltd, London.
Reprinted by permission, for use only in connection with the examinations of the Royal Schools of Music. All enquiries for this piece apart from the examinations should be addressed to Boosey & Hawkes Music Publishers Ltd, The Hyde, Edgware Road, London NW9 6JN.